TERRY O'NEILL is one of the world's most collected photographers with work hanging in national art galleries and private collections worldwide. From presidents to pop stars, he has photographed the frontline of fame for over six decades.

O'Neill began his career at the birth of the 1960s. While other photographers concentrated on earthquakes, wars and politics, O'Neill realised that youth culture was a breaking news story on a global scale and began chronicling the emerging faces of film, fashion and music who would go on to define the Swinging Sixties.

By 1965 he was being commissioned by the biggest magazines and newspapers in the world. No other living photographer has embraced the span of fame in the same way, capturing the icons of our age from Winston Churchill to Nelson Mandela, Frank Sinatra to Amy Winehouse, Audrey Hepburn and Brigitte Bardot, as well as five James Bonds from Sean Connery to Daniel Craig.

He photographed the Beatles and the Rolling Stones when they were still struggling young bands in 1963 and pioneered backstage reportage photography with David Bowie, Elton John, The Who and Chuck Berry, and his images have adorned historic rock albums, movie posters and international magazine covers. Currently, Terry is concentrating on revisiting his enormous archive and travelling around the world exhibiting his work.

He recently published the book *Terry O'Neill Opus* and *Terry O'Neill's Rock 'n' Roll Album*. See www.iconicimages.net

BREAKING STONES

1963 - 1965
A BAND ON THE BRINK OF SUPERSTARDOM

**PHOTOGRAPHS BY
TERRY O'NEILL & GERED MANKOWITZ**

ICONIC IMAGES
FINE ART ARCHIVES PUBLISHING CREATIVE

CEO, Iconic Images
Robin Morgan

Editor
Carrie Kania

Design Director
Stephen Reid

Production
Mariona Vilaros
Victoria Schofield

www.iconicimages.net

ACC EDITIONS

Publisher, ACC Editions
James Smith

Editor
Andrew Whittaker

Design
Craig Holden

Production
Jane Emeny

www.antiquecollectorsclub.com

INTRODUCTION

By Robin Morgan

In the early 1960s, the world was undergoing extraordinary social upheaval triggered by post-war prosperity and adolescent defiance; the tectonic plates of class, money, and power were colliding, and socioreligious rules were crumbling.

The new heroes of art, film, literature, and music were working-class boys and girls. Before 1963, youth was largely acquiescent and acquisitive. After 1963, they were impossible to ignore. They were catered to. They were marketed to. They were listened to. They were heard.

The Rolling Stones began their career during these fateful early years of the 1960s. Friends Mick Jagger and Keith Richards bonded over their mutual admiration of electric blues music from Chicago and wanted to play music like Muddy Waters and Howlin' Wolf. Along with Bill Wyman, Charlie Watts, Brian Jones and for a short time Ian Stewart, the Stones started to play the small clubs in London and quickly caught the eye of Andrew Loog Oldham, who in turn would become their manager. The rest, as they say, is history.

Two young photographers bore witness to the emergence of one of the greatest bands that would ever exist. In only a few short years, 1963-1965, Terry O'Neill and Gered Mankowitz, themselves just barely in their 20s, would capture singular moments of music history by simply being in the right place at the right time. O'Neill's iconic shots of a group of young "working musicians" carrying their suitcases down Tin Pan Alley, to Mankowitz's photos of the band on tour in America, would come to symbolise the youth, the times and the spirit of that age and how much fun it all looked. As Keith Richards so famously put it, "Suddenly you are on, up there onstage, and before you know it young ladies are throwing their underwear at you. A year earlier you couldn't get laid."

Breaking Stones: A Band on the Brink of Superstardom, featuring the photography of Terry O'Neill and Gered Mankowitz, is a celebration of that time; when the bands were young, when the music was loud and when the camera was there to capture every moment.

TERRY O'NEILL

Photographs 1963-1965

Terry O'Neill at work with the Rolling Stones

" When we arrived in Richmond to see this new band, late, there was a crowd of kids outside the Station Hotel who couldn't get in – the place was packed full. The noise was already fantastic... It was one of those Bo Diddley songs with a Bo Diddley beat. I'd never heard anything like it in a live act. I'd never felt anything like it. The place shook, everyone in the audience was wet with sweat, the sound was bouncing off the walls, throbbing, utterly irresistible. It lifted me up and swept me along, song after song. After the gig, as the crowd melted away, I hung around and was introduced to the Rolling Stones. Brian, the most intense character, was the chattiest, doing a PR job on me. 'What can you do for us?' he asked. What could I say? Anything they wanted, really. When I got back to the office that Wednesday, I sat down to write the article having the distinct feeling that I should be very careful in what I said. It was the first time I could remember a feature article written in *New Record Mirror* about an act that didn't yet have a record. *New Record Mirror* hit the streets in May with the Rolling Stones article on page two and that afternoon three or four major record companies phoned me to find out where they could contact the group "

**Norman Jopling,
music journalist**

THE ROLLING STONES — GENUINE R & B!

Originally published in the *New Record Mirror*, May 11, 1963

As the trad scene gradually subsides, promoters of all kinds of teen-beat entertainment heave a long sigh of relief that they have found something to take its place. It's Rhythm and Blues, of course — the number of R&B clubs that have sprung up is nothing short of fantastic.

One of the best-known — and one of the most successful to date — is at the Station Hotel, Kew Road, in Richmond, just on the outskirts of London. There, on Sunday evenings, the hip kids throw themselves about to the new "jungle music" like they never did in the more stinted days of trad.

And the combo they writhe and twist to is called the Rollin' Stones. Maybe you've never heard of them — if you live far away from London the odds are you haven't.

But by gad you will! The Rollin' Stones are probably destined to be the biggest group in the R&B scene if it continues to flourish. And by the looks of the Station Hotel, Richmond, flourish is merely an understatement considering that three months ago only fifty people turned up to see the group. Now club promoter, bearded Giorgio Gomelsky, has to close the doors at an early hour — over four hundred R&B fans crowd the hall.

And the fans who do come quickly lose all their inhibitions and proceed to contort themselves to the truly exciting music of the boys — who put heart and soul into their performances.

The fact is that, unlike all the other R&B groups worthy of the name, the Rollin' Stones have a definite visual appeal. They aren't the Jazzmen who were doing trad eighteen months back and who have converted their act to keep up with the times. They are genuine R&B fanatics themselves, and they sing and play in a way that one would expect more from a coloured U.S. R&B team than a bunch of wild, exciting white boys who have the fans screaming — and listening — to them.

Line-up of the group is Mick Jagger, lead vocal and harmonica and student at the London School of Economics. The fierce backing is supplied by Brian Jones, guitar and harmonica, and also spokesman and leader of the group. He's an architect, while Keith Richards, guitar, is an art student. The other three members of the group are Bill Wyman, bass guitar, Ian Stewart, piano and maracas, and drummer Charles Watts.

Record-wise, everything is in the air, but a disc will be forthcoming. It will probably be the group's own adaptation of the Chuck Berry number 'Come On' (featured on Chuck's new Pye LP). The number goes down extremely well in the club session on Sundays — other Chuck Berry numbers that are in the group's repertoire are 'Down The Road Apiece' and 'Bye Bye Johnny' — which is one of the highlights of the act.

Even though the boys haven't dead-certain plans for a disc, they do have dead-certain plans for a film. For club promoter Giorgio is best known as a film producer and has made several imaginative films dealing with the music scene. But for the Rollin' Stones film, there are some truly great shots of the team in action, singing and performing 'Pretty Thing,' the Bo Diddley number. The film itself lasts for twenty minutes and will be distributed with a main feature film.

The group are actually mad about Bo Diddley, although pianist Ian is the odd man out. Diddley numbers they perform are 'Crawdad,' 'Nursery Rhyme,' 'Road Runner,' 'Mona' and, of course, 'Bo Diddley.'

They can get the sound that Bo gets too — no mean achievement. The group themselves are all red-hot when it comes to U.S. beat discs. They know their R&B numbers inside out and have a repertoire of about eighty songs, most of them are the numbers which every R&B fan in the country knows and loves.

The boys are confident that, if they make a disc, it should do well. They are also confident about their own playing, although on Sundays at the end of the session they are dead-beat. That's because on Sunday afternoons they also play the R&B session at the Ken Colyer club.

But despite the fact that their R&B has a superficial resemblance to rock'n'roll, fans of the hit parade music would not find any familiar material performed by the Rollin' Stones. And the boys do not use original material. "After all," they say, "can you imagine a British-composed R&B number — it just wouldn't make it."

One group that thinks a lot of the Rollin' Stones are The Beatles. When they came down to London the other week, they were knocked out by the group's singing. They stayed all the evening at the Station Hotel listening to the group pound away. And now they spread the word around so much in Liverpool that bookings for the group have been flooding in — including several at the famed Cavern.

All this can't be bad for the R&B group who have achieved the American sound better than any other group over here. And the group that in all likelihood will soon be the leading R&B performers in the country...

Norman Jopling

Norman Jopling was a young reporter writing about rhythm & blues for Britain's *New Record Mirror*, one of the papers covering the music scene in the early 1960s. Asked to go see and write-up a piece about this new band called "The Rollin' Stones," Jopling wrote an article that would become a landmark in music journalism and help launch their career

Terry O'Neill asked the band to bring suitcases to the photoshoot because he wanted to convey the feeling of a real working-class, travelling band

❝ Terry O'Neill took this picture of us in Soho, we are these boys walking down the street, 'Oh look at these sharp kids.' We all have the Beatles boots on. First time we made substantial cash we all went down to the store and bought new guitars and Beatle boots. That was the kicks. That was it. You've made it! I had a brand new suitcase. It was the very first suitcase I ever owned, and we used it in the shoot ❞

Keith Richards

By Terry O'Neill

My career just started only a few years back before I met the Rolling Stones. I was the youngest of the photographers on Fleet Street and the editors knew I loved music. When the papers printed photos of the Beatles and the papers sold, I was the one they went to for more. It was Andrew Loog Oldham who called me up and asked me to have a look at this new band he was managing. I went to see them perform down in Richmond at The Crawdaddy Club. Well, you could tell right away that these guys were different. I could see they were really cool. Andrew wanted publicity for them and my editor wanted more bands.

They were young and still trying to figure out what their image was going to be. They first started off in suits, really clean cut like, then they moved towards being more themselves in front of the camera – the more successful they got, they more they felt comfortable about being themselves. I took them to the park, walked them around Soho and into Tin Pan Alley to photograph them near the studios there. I went backstage a lot with them while they were shooting television shows. At that time, like the papers, producers knew that the bands brought in the viewers and that's what everyone wanted. I got some great shots of them just hanging out backstage, getting ready to go on, having a last-minute hair cut, eating at the canteen. Just acting like a bunch of young 20-something-year-old boys. I used to go to a club at the back of Leicester Square, that's where all the young people used to go. And I used to sit there with the Beatles and the Rolling Stones, joking about what job they'd do after this. We all thought it was going to be over, we couldn't believe we had it so good. The young really were given the chance to do things and we grabbed it.

I didn't realise what an impact they were having until I went to Hollywood in 1964 on assignment. Here I was taking photos of legends like Fred Astaire and all they wanted to talk about was the Rolling Stones!

"When I sent the Stones photographs to my picture editor, he went berserk. 'They're ugly – get me a pretty band like the Beatles'"
Terry O'Neill

"The Stones just wanted to be very casual and they were the first really cool dressers; dressing down, creating their own laid-back, we-don't-give-a-damn style. And it wasn't contrived. They were the real poster boys of this revolution that was taking place – a revolution in identity and individuality"
Terry O'Neill

“ The first time we got a big article in the *Record Mirror,* I sat on the train with the magazine open on my lap expecting someone to notice. I was so proud of it ”
Bill Wyman

“I didn't have to work too hard.
They were just immediately cool”
Terry O'Neill

O'Neill took the band over to Tin Pan Alley, legendary home of Britain's music scene since 1911. Publications such as *New Musical Express* and *Melody Maker* started there and artists such as David Bowie, The Kinks and Black Sabbath all recorded at studios nearby. Today, a Blue Plaque marks the significance of this historic spot

"I don't remember where these pictures were taken, but I do remember the rubbish pink blanket they sat on. I'm pretty sure we ended up only reprinting these shots in black-and-white"
Terry O'Neill

Often times, locations were chosen just to attract attention. Public places, like Regent's Park, were perfect for drawing a crowd of onlookers to cause a stir

❝ You have to remember, they were a young band and Andrew (Loog Oldham, manager) had them working around the clock saying 'yes' to everything that was being offered. They were touring, being interviewed, recording, rehearsing seven days a week. So when we did photo shoots, I just took them around London ❞
Terry O'Neill

The musicians the newspapers and magazines were covering in 1963 all had a very clean look, including the Beatles and the Dave Clark Five. Often times, the band members would look like they were wearing uniforms of a smart jacket and trousers. In early press photos, the Rolling Stones tried to emulate these bands and only came into their own style and look later on as they gained more confidence. Andrew Loog Oldham also knew that delivering a "competing look" and style would be great for their image

“ I got a bunch of office girls to drape themselves over the boys, and put them on the banks of the Thames or up against graffiti, which made them look even edgier in those days. Dangerous was what I was looking for, because they kind of were – rebellious, different ”
Terry O'Neill

“ Terry would say, 'Let's throw a few dolly birds into the photo.' I always had a girlfriend somewhere but they always got fed up with me ”
Keith Richards

" Everything happened quickly. But you had to be quick in those days because there was so much going on and you could get lost in the rush "
Mick Jagger

❝ Nobody knew at the time (that) 1963 was a pivotal year. There was a whiff in the air, and I think Terry O'Neill probably felt it as much as I did, but from different angles. Terry was behind the lens, everywhere, always ❞
Keith Richards

“ At the time, it was really Brian's band. He was the man running the Stones. It was only years later that Keith and Mick would start to take centre stage ”
Terry O'Neill

"Andrew Loog Oldham was a great manager for them. And that's what the band needed – someone their age who loved their music and wanted to be number one. Andrew was – and still is – ahead of his time. He just knew what to do and where to take them. He never stopped hustling and pushing and networking and making things happen for the Stones. Keith's right when he says he was the sixth Stone"
Terry O'Neill

> It was a pressure cooker. There was no time off in those days. For three or four years we maybe had ten days or two weeks off in the whole year. At that age you've got non-stop energy and if things are working out and you're on the trail of something, you don't really notice how hard it is

Keith Richards

" People said we were copying the Beatles. Nonsense. They were tidy and we were scruffy. They were nice boys – we weren't "

Bill Wyman

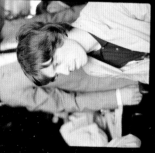

Newspapers like *Melody Maker* and *New Musical Express* were required reading for anyone interested in music.
How you looked and how you were presented on the page became increasingly important in the making of a band

> I was able to go with the band everywhere – backstage, on studio sets, even in the press waiting rooms. I think they got used to me hanging around

Terry O'Neill

At Andrew's request, Terry would often join the band backstage and at rehearsals for television appearances.
He was given all-access to take photos of the band in the most casual settings

"I didn't try to be cool. I didn't think about it. I think the minute you think about being cool, you ain't. I know a cool guy when I see him"
Keith Richards.

Radio phone interviews were part of the job and in-between photo sessions and rehearsals, the band would answer questions for anyone who had them

" I wasn't trying to be rebellious in those days; I was just being me. I wasn't trying to push the edge of anything. I'm being me and ordinary, the guy from suburbia who sings in this band **"**
Mick Jagger

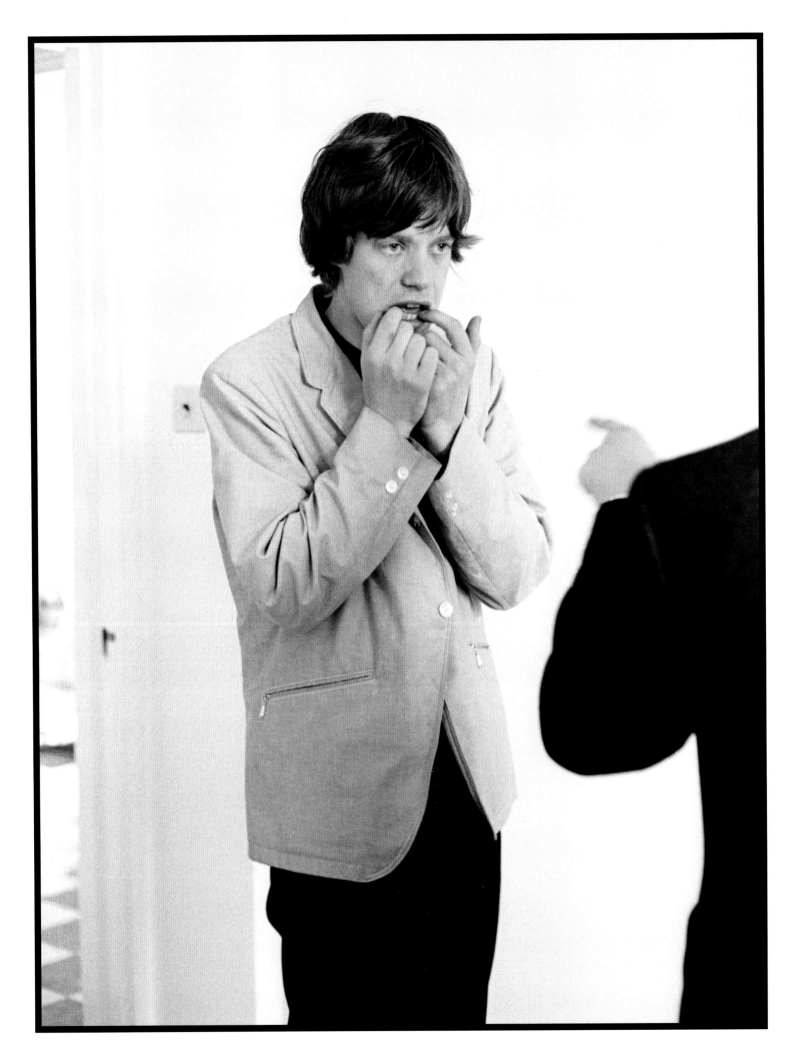

"People say I made the Stones.
I didn't. They were there already.
They only wanted exploiting. They
were all bad boys when I found them.
I just brought out the worst in them"
Andrew Loog Oldham

TAKE A MIDDLE-CLASS VALUE, STAND IT ON ITS HEAD: YOU'VE GOT A "STONE"

Originally published in the *Evening Standard*, 11 May, 1964

PARENTS DO NOT LIKE the Rolling Stones. They do not want their sons to grow up like them; they do not want their daughters to marry them.

Never have the middle-class virtues of neatness, obedience and punctuality been so conspicuously lacking as they are in the Rolling Stones. The Rolling Stones are not the people you build empires with; they are not the people who always remember to wash their hands before lunch.

They are five young men of almost frightening aspect whose music is exciting but untuneful.

"We're a pretty horrible looking bunch," they say comfortably.

Nobody disagrees.

Parents feel cheated. Just when the Beatles had taught them that pop music was respectable. Just when they were beginning to understand. What happens? Their children develop a passion beyond the comprehension of everybody for these five young men.

MORONS?

The Beatles are cheerful, witty, intelligent and above all, nice. Can the same be said for the Rolling Stones?

"People," said one of their managers nonchalantly, "are always asking me if they're morons."

It is their very deficiencies that have, in five months, made the Stones – as they are known to intimates – take second place only to the Beatles. They are not a serious challenge but they have a very important person, namely the floating fan, solidly behind them.

Mother and daughter cannot worship at the same shrine. The moment that the mothers, and fathers, and politicians, and employers, and foreigners, and Ella Fitzgerald, and crowned heads grew to love the Beatles, the floating fan went over to the Stones.

This defection had something to do with the fact that the Beatles have grown too famous. I remember that when they made their first record lots of little girls in Liverpool wouldn't buy it for fear they would grow too famous and go away and…

The girls long to reform them [the Stones], cut their hair, stop them smoking. They imagine, quite wrongly, that they have leukemia and need nursing. They also, which is very strange, want to wear their clothes.

Boys like the Stones partly because of their music which is rhythm and blues and the smartest new thing and partly because they would be Stones if they dared. They would have a Peter Pan existence with no grown-ups bossing them around…

RACE

[Brian Jones] left Cheltenham Grammar School prematurely. He became obsessed by the music.

Bill Wyman, the married one, bears a marked resemblance to both Charles I and Charles II.

If apes were handsome, they would look like Charlie Watts. His managers think Steve McQueen looks like him. He is a bit of a dandy.

Keith Richards is the only one I would have ever dreamed of making into a pop singer. He has a pert Oliver Twist face and likes doing potty things like building walls round people's front doors in the night.

Though they are very pleasant to meet they make little effort to charm their audience. They are detached, distant, almost abstracted. They just stand there, jigging vaguely about, wearing whatever clothes they happened to get up in that morning.

"We can't wear uniforms," they say, "it would feel like the army." It's very much a case of "like us or lump us."

They are all very skinny and, though you wouldn't guess it, quite keen on clothes. The trouble is they don't actually finish putting them on. A natty lilac shirt, clean and starchy, will be left undone at the cuffs. The dark suit will be well-tailored but worn minus the tie. This gives them a dishevelled aimless look.

SCRUFFY

They hate to be thought grubby. Scruffy, yes; grubby, no. They say they wash quite a lot.

"The Rolling Stones are not just a group; they are a way of life." This is one of the wilder statements on the sleeve of their record.

I don't know about their being a way of life, but sometimes I strongly suspect they're a figment of our imagination.

© Maureen Cleave, 1964

"Do not let your daughter marry a Rolling Stone" was unquestionably the work of Andrew Loog Oldham. Knowing exactly the way to maximize publicity, he wanted to set the Rolling Stones apart from all the other new bands springing up in London in the early 1960s. He knew the "bad boy" reputation would be the perfect antidote to the clean-cut image of the Beatles

“ We got recognised after the TV show. It was kinda exciting because it was all pretty girls. Girls started to ask for autographs ”
Bill Wyman

"Mick didn't have an instrument so he seemed to use his body – make it work with the music, act out the song, striking poses, pouting, pushing himself. He was very charismatic already. He was a showman. Other bands, the guy just stood there and sang. Mick moved"
Terry O'Neill

" We would have made it without the TV show, but it made us known countrywide, and then we got offers to play outside London. Before that we were just a band in a jazz club "

Bill Wyman

Thank Your Lucky Stars was a weekly television show that ran in Britain from 1961 to 1966. The program showcased the latest hit records. New bands would appear on the show, often making their debut television appearance. The Rolling Stones did just that, appearing for the first time on 7 July, 1963, and would appear two more times that year

Ready Steady Go! was another weekly music program that aired in Britain from 1963 until 1966. The Rolling Stones made their debut appearance on the show on 23 August, 1963, and appeared again a few months later

❝ I was invited to come along to all different types of television shows and snapped shots during rehearsals, backstage – you name it. It wasn't rare to have that much access in the early 1960s, certainly not like today where everything is over-controlled ❞
Terry O'Neill

“ This was really the first decade and the first group of musicians who realised what television could do for them. If a band appeared on a popular show, you can bet their next gig sold out. It was as simple as that ”
Terry O'Neill

Backstage always presented the band with the opportunity to meet other entertainers. Here Keith Richards and Mick Jagger meet up with Kenny Lynch backstage on *Thank Your Lucky Stars*

Lionel Bart, pictured here with the band and Andrew, is probably best known for creating the book and lyrics for the musical *Oliver!*. Bart was instrumental in the early days of the Rolling Stones and helped Andrew fund two companies: Forward Sounds to handle recording projects and Forward Music to handle songs. Marianne Faithfull was the first Forward artist

"You can see by the photos how comfortable they started to get in front of the camera. In the very early shots, they are still standing up straight, grinning away. The more time I spent with them, and as their fame started to grow, they just relaxed more and became the band we know today"
Terry O'Neill

The hooded, Parka-style coat was considered fashionable thanks to the Mods in the 1950s and 60s, although the Mods would often unbutton and detach the fur hood

❝ Mick turned up in a coat with a fur hood and a pair of corduroy trousers, and pulled faces ❞
Terry O'Neill

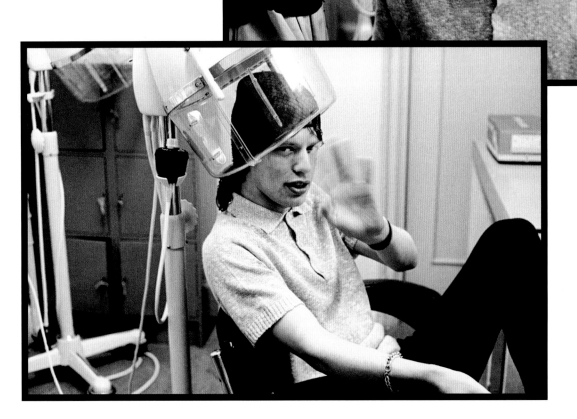

"I was backstage with them mucking about: Mick under a hair dryer, Keith shaving from a light socket, Brian messing with Bill's hair, Andrew and Keith sharing a cup of tea. I shot some great reportage that day"
Terry O'Neill

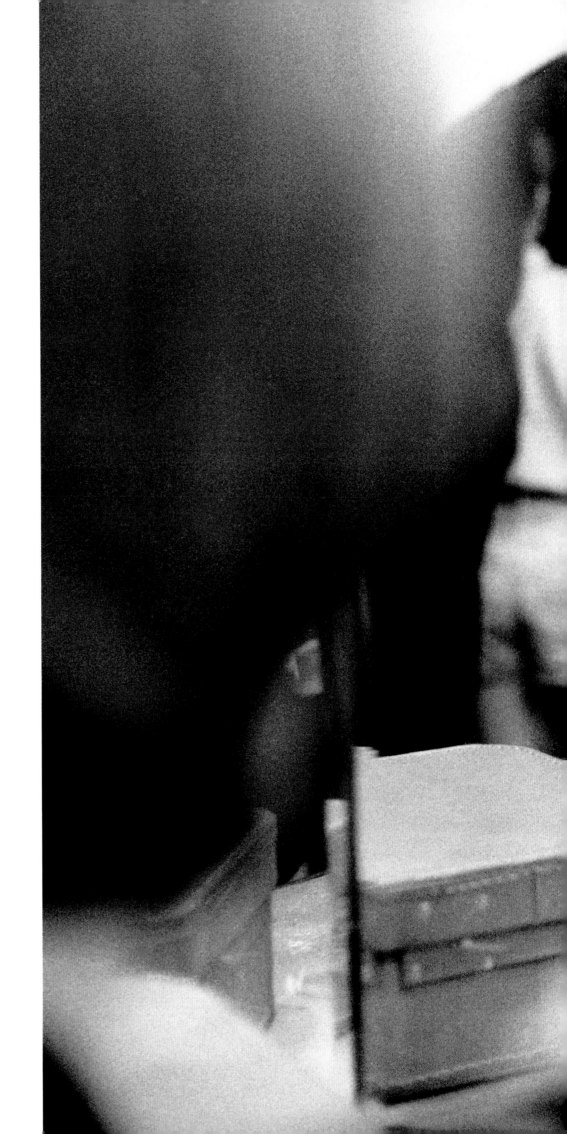

Most bands at the time had a uniform look, but the Rolling Stones broke all the rules and each member developed their own distinct style

“ A lot of us were really into our clothes. We liked to dress smart – Italian suits, kind of cool and continental, single-breasted jackets, plain knitted neckties. The Stones were really the first cool dressers. They created their own style ”
Terry O'Neill

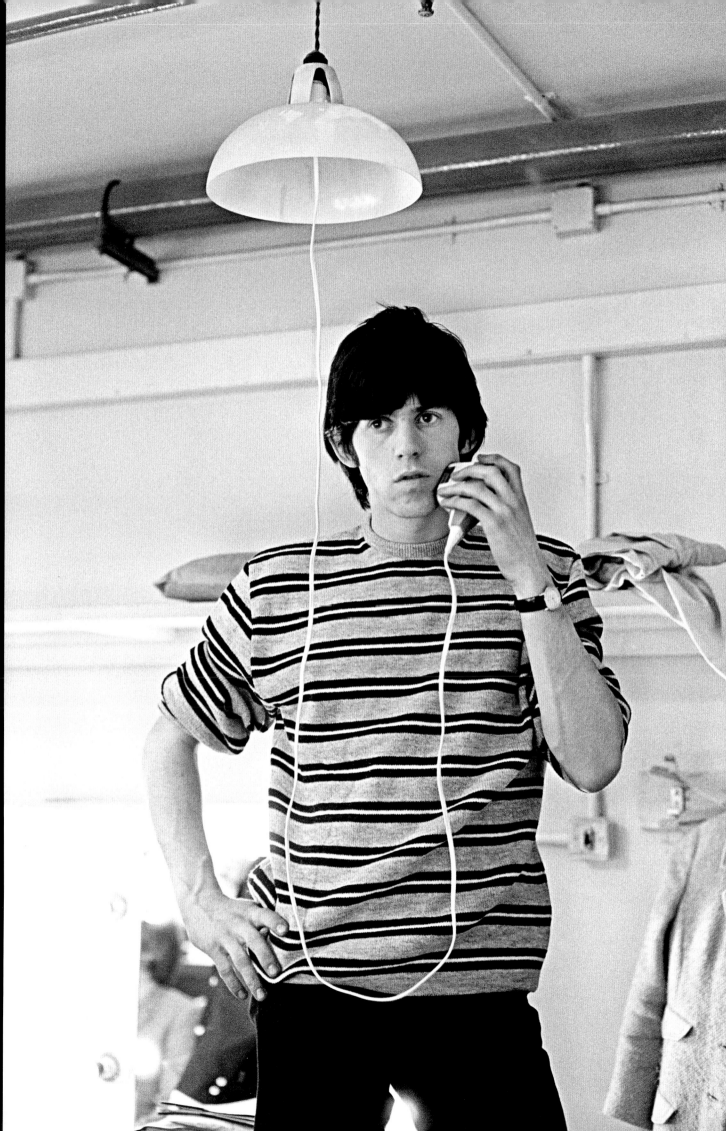

“ Brian wanted to be different to the rest of us, but he didn't know who he wanted to be ”
Keith Richards

Charlie Watts was holding down a job with an advertising firm during the day and playing drums at night when he finally quit his job and joined the Stones full time

❝ I knew there was something special very early on. Most bands start very enthusiastically and gradually audiences drop off. This lot was totally different ❞
Charlie Watts

Peter Sellers famously quipped on *The Goon Show* in 1954: "Lunch is now being served in the BBC canteen. Doctors are on standby...". It didn't matter to the Rolling Stones who happily enjoyed any meal they were able to grab as they waited for their next media appearance

66 The Sixties was an incredible time. Young people took over, creating their own cultural landscape on stage, in music, fashion and on the film set. I was lucky. Seriously lucky. I was in the right place at the right time 99
Terry O'Neill

GERED MANKOWITZ

Photographs 1965

Gered on the plane, snapshot by Mick Jagger

552 B

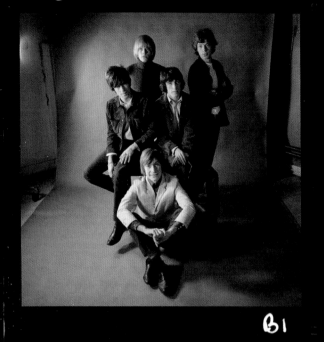
B1

B4

B2

B5

B3

B6

> We were all entering into something that we didn't know what it was, how long it would last, or how special it was. We just took it day by day. It wasn't intentional. We didn't plan to be rebels, and neither did the fashion people or photographers. They were just doing their normal jobs with new ideas. It wasn't pre-planned or organised – it just happened. Everyone tries to make things happen now. We weren't trying to make things happen. That's why it will never happen again. We just wanted to play the music
>
> **Bill Wyman**

Andrew Loog Oldham was also working with a new singer named Marianne Faithfull, and it was Gered Mankowitz's classic "Faithfull at the pub" photograph that inspired Oldham to ask the young photographer to work with the Rolling Stones. Already a fan of the band from seeing them on television earlier in the year, he met them at his studio in Mason's Yard, London, at the beginning of 1965

by Gered Mankowitz

In 1965, the Rolling Stones took control of their destiny, hand-in-hand with Andrew Loog Oldham.

I was working with Alec Murray, a marvellous man and a great photographer. I went to Paris with him for the collections, but the experience just turned me off fashion. I just didn't want to be that sort of photographer. In 1964, I met Marianne Faithfull socially and immediately wanted to photograph her. She was managed by Andrew Loog Oldham. I photographed her on Wimbledon Common and in the recording studio. But it was the shot of Marianne inside The Salisbury, a pub in St. Martins Lane, that got Andrew's attention. He asked if I would shoot with the Stones who he also managed. I met with the band in Andrew's office in Ivor Court at the end of 1964. We really hit it off and, I admit, I was already a fan just from seeing them on television. We scheduled a photo session for early 1965 at my little studio in Mason's Yard. Because they were always so busy touring and recording I realised that they needed a lot of material. I had them for a few hours and we shot various set-ups in the studio and outside at different points around the studio. Andrew and the band were really happy with the results. Those first Mason's Yard shots were used on a tour program, record covers, press – and I was only 18. I think my youthful energy and lack of photo experience suited the Stones and we just clicked.

A few months later, I got a call from Andrew. Did I want to go to America with the Stones and photograph the tour? I was just bowled over! It was pretty exciting to be asked to go to America, my first trip there; it was the land of our dreams. All I wanted to do was to focus on music photography. Music was my world and everyone in it was around my age. Working with the Stones really underscored my focus and gave me opportunities to pursue a rock music photo career.

When the time came to head for the States, it was just the band, me and Ian 'Stu' Stewart on the plane to New York. I went with the band everywhere. Up to a point, I was treated like a member of the band.

I'm asked all the time why I don't have more shots of them just hanging out at the hotel, or more behind-the-scenes other than the backstage photos. There's a reason for that. Andrew said that when the guys are back at the hotel, that's private. I respected their privacy – in those days, it was still important. That's why you don't see pictures of them on the beach or messing around. And I didn't take photos for myself. Maybe I should have, and disregarded what he said. But it seemed like the right thing to do at the time. When they would pack up their instruments I'd pack up my camera. I suppose in hindsight it was really stupid of me, but blame it on youthfulness and inexperience! The other reason Andrew didn't want me to do that stuff was because Dezo Hoffman toured with the Beatles in America earlier and he had taken a lot of posed and stylised photos of the band. The "having a bit of fun" shots of them leap frogging on the beach. Andrew was just appalled by that. I think he thought that sort of showbiz element was absolutely not for the Stones. That was not the image he or the band wanted.

Touring in those days was as basic as you can get. That's something people completely forget about. There was no sound crew, no lighting, and no set. But it was the first tour where they had their own plane, which was needed because of the distances between dates. When we would land in a city in the middle of the night, a couple of cars would pick us up and Stu would load the equipment into a truck that was also waiting. Driven to the motel, we would crash until heading for the venue the next day. The gigs were so badly lit; it was really difficult to get a good exposure. You have to remember, most of these concert venues were not designed for rock bands. They were sports venues not theatres, so Mick would often be in the only spotlight and the rest of the band in semi-darkness. That's why I tried to shoot into the light just to get something atmospheric. But the more Mick danced around, the more the light followed him. That's how it was in those days. No one knew how to produce a rock show. This is just a few years after Elvis was performing on a flat-bed truck. Promoters had very little experience of this sort of thing. Lighting designed for a sporting event is not the same lighting needed for the Rolling Stones.

I was allowed to go anywhere on stage as long as I didn't get in Mick's way. I would sometimes shoot from behind Charlie and take photos over the amps just to try to capture Mick's movements, and the atmosphere. A lot of it was really luck whether or not the pictures came out. Photographically it was a frustrating assignment, mainly because I wasn't technically very confident yet, and the lighting was so poor. I'd send over bundles of film to the studio in London for processing and they would send the proofs over to Andrew. I got a little feedback but I didn't see any of the photos until I got back.

I always say that the most basic pub band today has better equipment than the Rolling Stones did back in 1965, even with a number one record. That tour was so incredibly topsy-turvy and chaotic. Everybody had seen the Beatles on Sullivan and there had been Johnny Ray, Elvis, Sinatra of course – but nobody performed like the Stones.

"They were just stacked randomly against a wall, and I saw this deep triangular shape and got the guys to pose for me at the other end of it. I knew that that was going to work for a record cover, if I was lucky enough to get it, because it gave natural places to put the band's name and the logo and all that stuff. That was crucial in those days because record covers weren't conceived or planned. When that shot was picked for the cover, it was a huge, huge breakthrough for me and confirmation that I was doing something right"

Gered Mankowitz

" You're sitting with some guys, and you're playing and you go, 'Oooh, yeah!' That feeling is worth more than anything. There's a certain moment when you realise that you've actually just left the planet for a bit and that nobody can touch you. You're elevated because you're with a bunch of guys that want to do the same thing as you. And when it works, baby, you've got wings "
Keith Richards

"Andrew Loog Oldham taking the piss out of the positions that photographers get themselves into!" Gered Mankowitz

❝ In those days the hardest thing to do was to record, and from a musician's point of view the most difficult thing was to break into a recording studio ❞
Keith Richards

At first, the Rolling Stones were essentially a covers band. Only after Andrew Loog Oldham strongly suggested that Mick and Keith start writing their own songs did the band finally reach the top of the charts. Oldham knew that the only way they were going to reach number one, like the Beatles, was to start penning — and recording — original songs

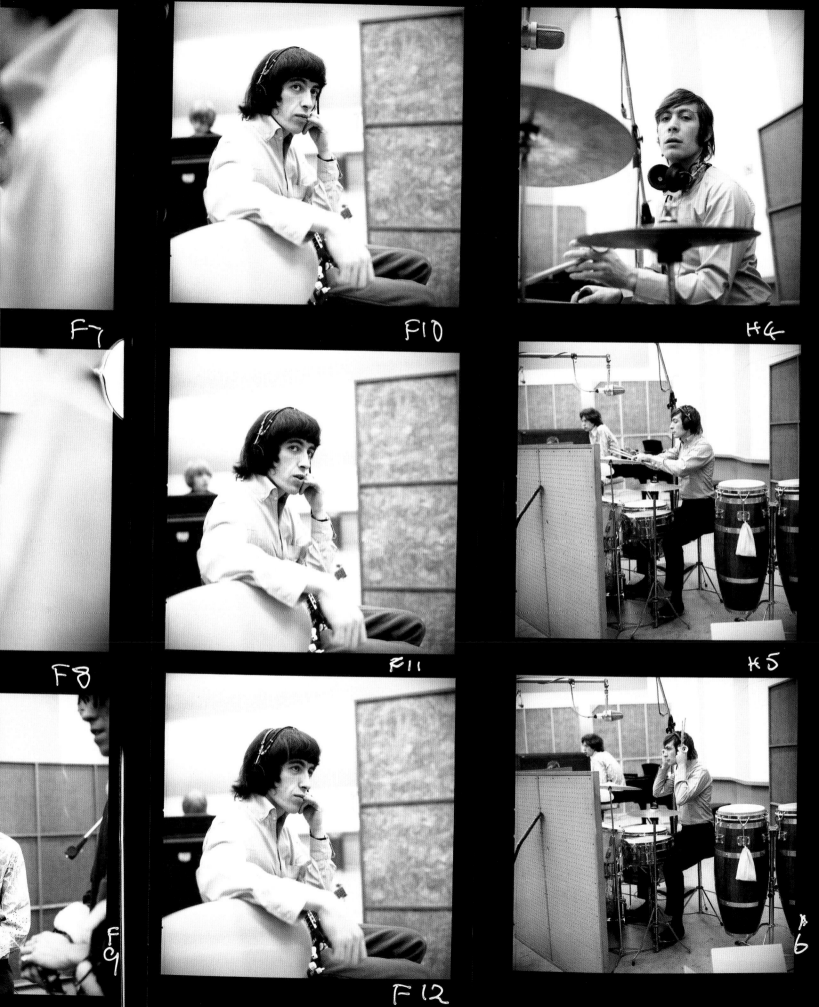

Gered Mankowitz not only captured the Stones at work, but also took memorable shots of the band during "in-between" moments. Girlfriends, like Anita Pallenberg, would often swing by the studio

> **"** One of the big differences with the Beatles and the Rolling Stones is the Beatles made it in America. The Rolling Stones were made by America. Once we got to America, we went, oh, wow, this is magic. We, the Rolling Stones, were home in the mecca of everything the band lived for **"**
> **Andrew Loog Oldham**

When asked if he wanted to go on tour to America with the Stones in the Fall of 1965, Mankowitz jumped at the chance.
He was only 19 and it was his first visit to the States. Outside a few candid shots like these, he decided
to put down his camera when the band put down their instruments. "I just didn't know not to.
My job on the tour was to take photos of them on stage. Their private life was private. And I respected that"

> **"** I was so young. But that youth brought an innocence and grittiness to my photography, something much more raw and naturalistic than the approach of other photographers who were shooting the band **"**
>
> **Gered Mankowitz**

Incredibly, this tour was their fourth to the States in under two years. And with each tour, the crowds got bigger

> In New York, a few limos met us at the airport to take us to the hotel. When we arrived, there were fans everywhere. Then they just swamped the car, climbing all over it, denting the roof. We were shouting 'Drive!' but no one knew what to do

Gered Mankowitz

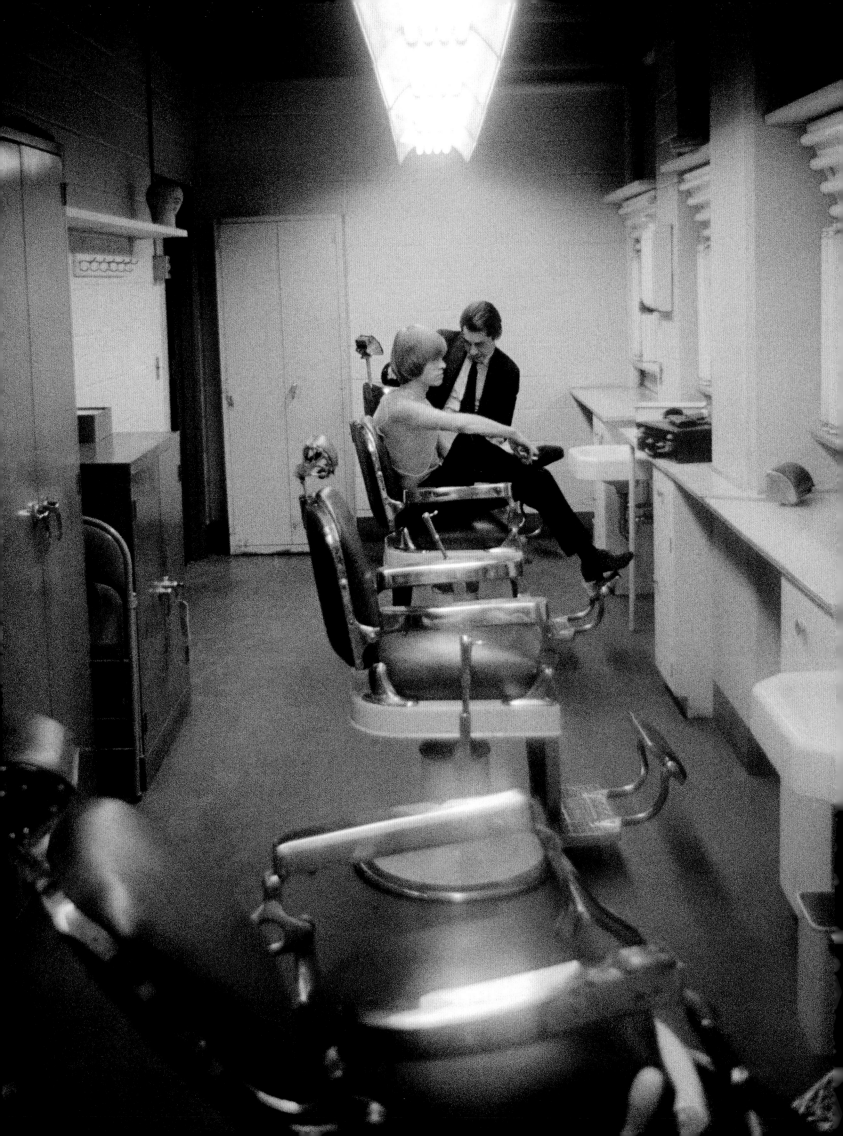

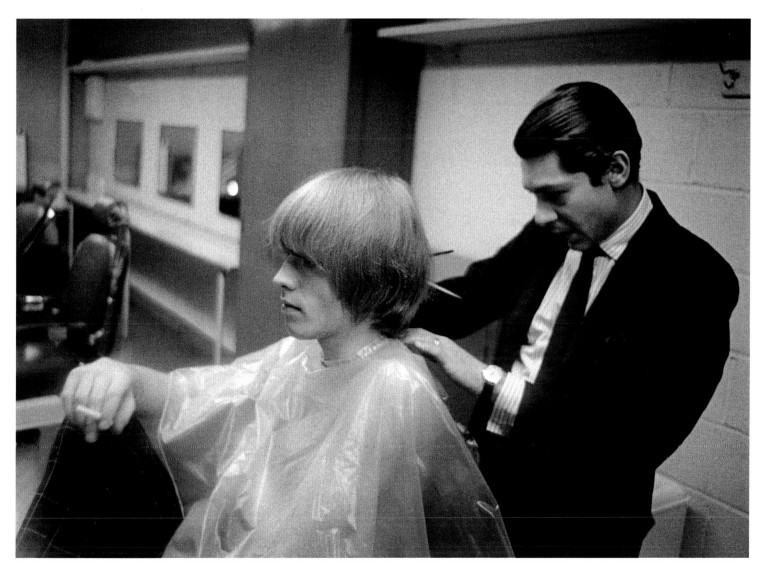

" Brian was always concerned about image, especially his hair. This was backstage before a taping of *Hullabaloo* (an American music variety show that ran from 1965-1966). I love the difference between the two hairstyles – almost shows how radical their look really was "
Gered Mankowitz

“ Music is language that doesn't speak particular words, it speaks in emotions, and if it's in the bones, it's in the bones ”
Mick Jagger

The dancing girls the television show provided were not necessarily the right match for the style of music the Stones would play

Like in the UK, television was a big part of the plan for a successful US invasion. Television shows like *Hullabaloo* knew that to attract the viewers, they needed to showcase the rising stars, especially the ones coming in from Britain

When the band hit the road, often they would play in venues better equipped for sports. Never mind, they made-do with their surroundings

❝ The Beatles looked like they were in show business, and that was the important thing. And the important thing for the Rolling Stones was to look as if they were not ❞
Andrew Loog Oldham

At just about every venue, someone – the police, security team, owner of the theatre, local promoter – would come backstage and have a word with the band about the crowd. It was clear even before the band took the stage that the fans were getting "too excited" and warnings were given not to encourage the screaming or dancing. Venues did not know how to handle a thousand or more screaming teenagers

" It was just me and the band and their roadie Ian Stewart, who had been part of the original Stones. Access wasn't an issue. I was treated like another Rolling Stone. The best thing, actually, was being on stage with them night after night. I was allowed to be on stage as long as I didn't get in Mick's way. They didn't have a lighting show, they didn't have a proper sound system. It was extremely crude and terribly low key in terms of packaging and presentation and equipment "
Gered Mankowitz

“ Mick never had a problem in front of an audience ”
Charlie Watts

"When the band arrived in Fort Worth, Texas, they discovered the stage was set up in the middle of the concert hall. Venues didn't send bands layouts or plans ahead of time, not like today. And there was no way they could just walk through the crowd to get to the stage. It would have been a riot, there wasn't enough security to protect them. The police were so twitchy with the crowd and no one had any sort of experience in dealing with this sort of thing. So a local armoured truck came around. We didn't mean for it to be dramatic, they just loaded themselves in the back, someone drove to the centre and let them out"
Gered Mankowitz

"Every band touring at that time was going through the same thing. That's how it was. The Stones had the best managers, agents, but when you go into a town, the town is run by the townspeople. The local sheriff, the local fire chief, the local health and safety committee. Then you have the local promoters who often times owned the theatre. It doesn't matter who you are or what number you are on the charts, it's their town. There were arguments backstage every night and we'd all tell them not to worry about the screaming, not to worry about the dancing. They just weren't experienced in handing this sort of phenomena" Gered Mankowitz

"The audiences were packed and much more boisterous – kids really – the police didn't know how to handle it. The first sign of screaming – and that's what the kids did – the moment the audience tried to stand up, the police or security team would be on them. If they appeared like they wanted to rush the stage, the show would be stopped. The police chief or fire chief would go up on stage and talk to the audience like a school master. 'If you don't stay in your seats, we're going to stop the show.' Then Mick would get back on the stage and shake his bum" Gered Mankowitz

At the first sign of screaming or dancing, in some towns, the police would stop the show and ask the audience to settle down

“ Touring like this was still new in 1965.
Every city had different rules ”
Gered Mankowitz

In many cities, fans were asked to remain seated. Afraid the show would stop, most decided to stay in their seats and scream

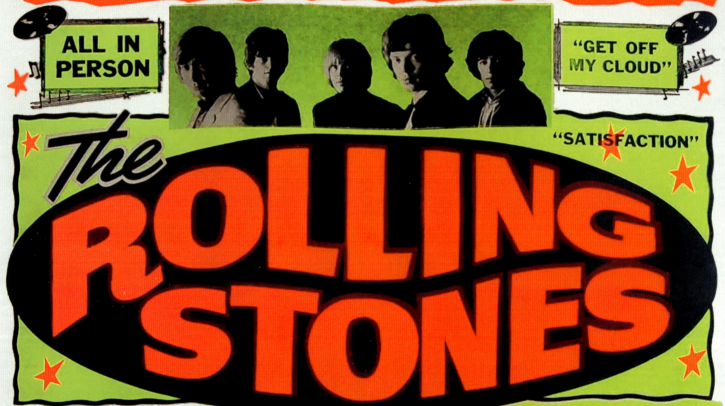

THE ROLLING STONES: THE GIRLS WAITED 8 HOURS, FINALLY MET THE STONES!

The US press had a field day reporting on this new British band travelling across the country. In some cities, they focused on reactions from a new powerful media-hungry group – the American teenager

Originally published in the *Detroit Free Press*, December, 1965.

Nobody's to get Valerie Stewart, 14, or Patricia Curtis, 13, off their clouds. The guys who put them up on Cloud 9 are the same ones who've been singing 'Get Off Of My Cloud' by the Rolling Stones.

Pat and Val won the Free Press' "Meet the Stones" contest and talked to the group last Friday before their Cobo Arena appearance.

But they almost didn't. And it took the girls from 1:15 p.m. until 9:15 p.m. until they did.

The meeting first was scheduled for Robin Seymour's Swingin' Time on the CKLW-TV show.

But the Stones didn't show. Everyone waited, waited, waited. And still no Stones.

Valerie, a ninth-grader at Marshall Jr. High, was all smiles and Pat, an eighth-grader in Romulus Jr. High, whispered: "I'm nervous."

But Robin didn't fail them, he put the girls on the show without any Stones. The singing group explained later it was a mix-up with their promoters that kept them away. Pat and Valerie, though, still had their chance to meet the Stones. CKLW arranged for the winners to go backstage at Cobo Arena.

Even with a letter of introduction and permission, getting through the stage door was harder than getting into LBJ's office. Finally inside, Val and Pat waited in a dressing room while the rest of the performers wandered in and out. But the Rockin' Ramrods and the Vibrations just weren't the Stones.

Then after almost a two-hour wait, THEY arrived – 15 minutes before they were to go on stage. Mick Jagger greeted the two girls who looked ready to faint. Mick signed their autograph books, posed for pictures with them, and then took the girls around to meet the other Stones.

Brian Jones, in brilliant red corduroy trousers, looked up at Valerie from the guitar he was tuning. "What's your name, luv?" he asked. "Val," she barely got out.

What Are Those Cuts?

I asked Mick about the cuts under his eyes. They were from things thrown on stage by enthusiastic fans. Why do they do it? "I suppose they want to touch us and can't," said Mick.

Did he like Detroit? "We wouldn't come here if we didn't like it."

I had read that the Stones usually were nasty to the press. I wanted to know why they were being so nice to us. Mick smiled. "I suppose those rumours are from people who don't know us."

How did the girls feel when it was all over? Said Val, "Great, I never thought I'd be in there." Pat exclaimed, "Wonderful, I can't get over it."

Who did Val dig the most? "Before, I never liked Mick. I liked Brian the best. Now I like Mick the best."

Would Pat's friends envy her? "I'm going to envy myself."

by Loraine Alterman

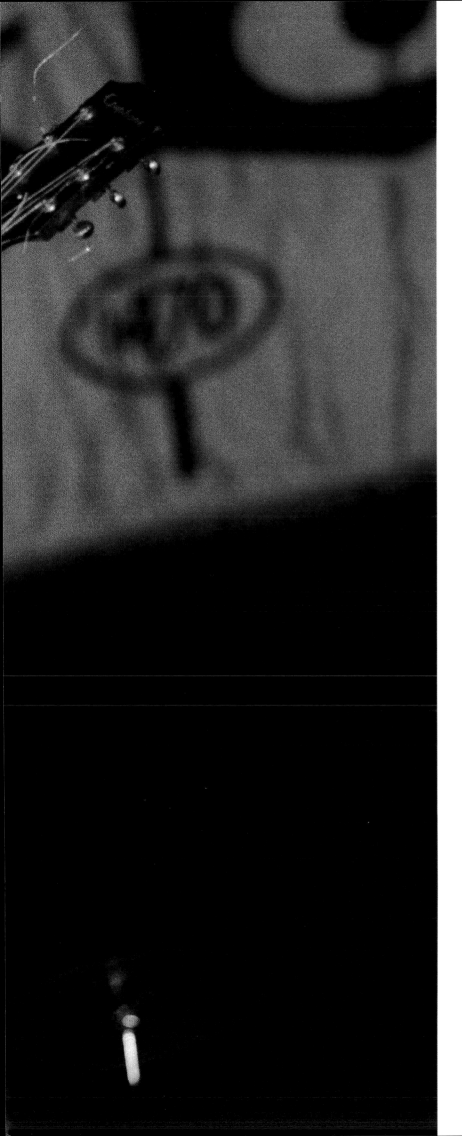

"Before the money and the pressure there was just enjoyment, just being there and part of the movement. I still feel the same way. Can't really rationalise about it but it was an amazing period. Thank God I was there"
Keith Richards

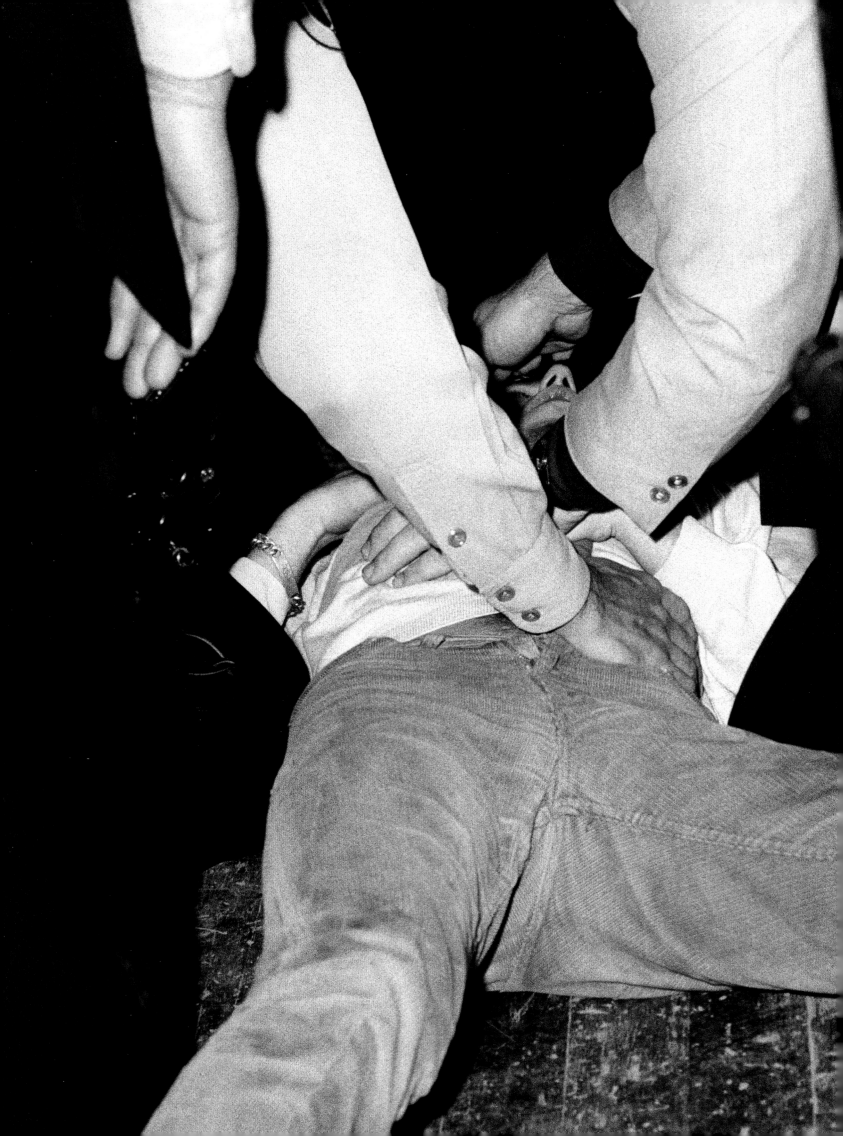

> " Yes, it's true and I witnessed it. Keith was electrocuted on the tour. It was the metal strings of the guitar touching the unearthed mike stand that caused the short circuit. It was terrifying. He was only out for a few minutes but it was still a horrible thing to see "
> **Gered Mankowitz**

"Get a shot," Allen Klein, famed American music promoter, said to Gered when Keith was electrocuted

F1
F4

F2
F5

F3
F6

❝ The lighting was so bad I couldn't actually take pictures. That's one of the reasons why I used to stand at the back and shoot out into the spotlight – to try to capture the atmosphere ❞
Gered Mankowitz

" The Mason's Yard sessions and this tour changed my life. I came off the road a better photographer – again, I was only 19 years old. 1965 opened my eyes "
Gered Mankowitz

> "I think the Rolling Stones have gotten a lot better. An awful lot better, I think. A lot of people don't, but I think they have, and to me that's gratifying. It's worth it"
> **Charlie Watts**

" They became kings of the road in very short order. Even success in the recording studio had to take second place and bow to the all-importance of the road. And just look at the result. What are the Stones doing now? They are on the road and it is theirs! "
Andrew Loog Oldham

BREAKING STONES

1963-1965
A BAND ON THE BRINK OF SUPERSTARDOM

**PHOTOGRAPHS BY
TERRY O'NEILL & GERED MANKOWITZ**

© 2016 Terry O'Neill, Gered Mankowitz

World copyright reserved

ISBN 978-1-85149-816-1

The rights of Iconic Images, Terry O'Neill and Gered Mankowitz to be identified as authors of this work have been asserted by them in accordance with the Copyright, Designs and Patents Act 1988

Introduction text © Robin Morgan
Images: front endpaper; pages 2-135 (except pages 12 and 78) © Iconic Images/Terry O'Neill
Images: pages 136-239 (except page 218); back endpaper © Bowstir Ltd./Gered Mankowitz
Images: page 12 and 78 © Getty Images

All rights reserved. No part of this publication may be reproduced, stored in a retrieval system, or transmitted in any form or by any means electronic, mechanical, photocopying, recording or otherwise, without the prior permission of the publisher

British Library Cataloguing-in-Publication Data
A catalogue record for this book is available from the British Library

Printed in China for ACC Editions, an imprint of ACC Art Books Ltd., Woodbridge, Suffolk, UK

Front cover: the Rolling Stones in Soho, London, 1963, photographed by Terry O'Neill.
Back cover: from Gered Mankowitz's first shoot with the Stones, outside his studio in Mason's Yard, London, 1965.

Grateful thanks to Andrew Loog Oldham for his words of wisdom and his iconic book
Stoned: A Memoir of London in the 1960s.
Also thanks to Norman Jopling for allowing reproduction of "The Rolling Stones – Genuine R&B" and for his book
Shake It Up Baby!: Notes from a Pop Music Reporter 1961-1972.
Acknowledgements also to *1963: The Year of the Revolution* by Robin Morgan and Ariel Leve,
published by It Books, an imprint of HarperCollins.
Thanks also to Barney Hoskyns and Rock's Backpages.

ACC EDITIONS

GERED MANKOWITZ was born in London in 1946, the first son of the author and screen writer Wolf Mankowitz and the psychotherapist Ann Mankowitz.

He left school devoid of any academic qualifications, aged 15, and served a short but intensive apprenticeship at Camera Press Ltd., having been inspired to pursue photography by the actor Peter Sellers. Gered established his first studio in Mason's Yard in 1963, in the very heart of 60s swinging London.

He met and photographed Marianne Faithfull in 1964, who was managed by the mercurial Andrew Loog Oldham, who also managed the Rolling Stones.

Gered started working with the Rolling Stones in 1965; he toured America with them and produced several album covers for the band. He continued working with them until 1967, by which time Gered was established as one of London's leading rock photographers. Early in 1967 Gered worked with The Jimi Hendrix Experience, producing during two sessions at his Mason's Yard studio images of Jimi that would go on to become some of the most iconic and widely known portraits of the great musician.

Over the past 50 years Gered has continued to work in the music business as well as contributing to many leading magazines and also taking prize-winning images for the advertising industry. Currently, Gered is concentrating on books and exhibitions as well as producing and selling prints in galleries all over the world. He recently published a retrospective book called *Gered Mankowitz: 50 Years of Rock and Roll Photography*. He is now based in Cornwall, where he is also a part-time lecturer at University College Falmouth. See www.mankowitz.com